The
Presidents
of the
United States

The Marshall Cavendish illustrated history of

The
Presidents
of the
United States

Written by
Ruth Oakley

Illustrated by
Steve Lucas and Tim Woodcock-Jones

MARSHALL CAVENDISH
New York · London · Toronto · Sydney

Library Edition Published 1990

© Marshall Cavendish Limited 1990
© DPM Services Limited 1990

Published by Marshall Cavendish Corporation
147, West Merrick Road
Freeport
Long Island
N.Y. 11520

Series created by Graham Beehag Book Design
Designed by Graham Beehag
Produced by DPM Services Limited

Library of Congress Cataloging-in-Publication Data

Oakley, Ruth.
  The Marshall Cavendish illustrated history of presidents of the United States / by Ruth Oakley
    p. cm.
  Includes indexes.
  Summary: Places each American preesident in a historical context and discusses his life, with an emphasis on his political activity and presidential term.
  ISBN 1-85435-144-3 (set)
  1. Presidents – United States – Biography – Juvenile literature. 2. United States – Politics and government – Juvenile literature.
[1. Presidents.] I. Title.
E176.8.025 1990
973'.0992 – dc20   89-17283
[B]   CIP
[920]   AC

Printed and bound in the United States of America by Lake Book Manufacturing Inc.

CONTENTS

Introduction

When Dwight D. Eisenhower won the presidential election of 1953, one of his first tasks was to end the Korean War. As a five-star general with a reputation for military victory during World War II, he had the prestige necessary to negotiate a peace treaty. Such a truce would not have been accepted if Truman had tried to suggest it. Eisenhower was then able to lead the United States through a period of peace, stability and prosperity for eight years. He made real efforts to reach an understanding with the Soviet leaders and to lessen the risks of nuclear war; he signed the first treaty to limit the testing of nuclear weapons. Yet, during his presidency, the nuclear arms race gathered momentum.

Eisenhower began to introduce legislation to enforce civil rights for blacks, which had been promised after the Civil War, but which had never been put into practice. He was prepared to use federal troops to enforce the desegregation of schools in Little Rock, Arkansas. The black protest movement, led at first by the non-violent Dr. Martin Luther King and later by others who were willing to use violence to gain their rights, continued its struggle through the presidencies of John F. Kennedy and Lyndon Johnson.

Kennedy and Johnson continued and increased the move toward social reform begun during Eisenhower's administration. Kennedy gave the United States the target of landing the first man on the moon, and Johnson, too, supported space exploration enthusiastically. Johnson and his wife, "Lady Bird," were active in conservation issues and concerned about the quality of life for all citizens.

Despite these high ideals and exciting technological developments, the sixties were also a period of violence for the U.S. at home and abroad. This violence entered most people's homes via their television screens. John F. Kennedy, Martin Luther King, and Robert Kennedy were all killed by gunmen. There were race riots in most major cities and anti-war demonstrations on university campuses. The

Vietnam War led to personal grief and tragedy for thousands of young men and their families, American and Vietnamese, and divided the American nation between those who thought the war was right and those who opposed it.

When Johnson refused to run for another term in 1968, he said, "I do not believe I can unite this country."

It was a task which remained for future leaders.

Eisenhower ended the Korean war.

7

DWIGHT D. EISENHOWER

(1890-1969)

Thirty-fourth President: 1953-1961

General Dwight D. Eisenhower came to the Presidency in 1953 as a famous soldier and a leader of world renown, although he was not a professional politician. He gave the impression of being capable and dependable, and his cheerful grin and friendly manner made people warm to him. A popular slogan of the time was "I like Ike."

Because he liked to play golf and bridge and go hunting and fishing, some people thought he did not take an active leadership role as president. This was an impression that he enjoyed creating. "Leadership is the ability to decide what is to be done and then to get others to want to do it," he said.

In fact, although he had chosen his cabinet very carefully and had confidence in their abilities, he took a close interest in the day-to-day concerns of both domestic and foreign policy. He had clear objectives, especially in foreign affairs. The control of nuclear arms and the development of peaceful uses of atomic energy, as well as America's relationship with the Soviet Union and the Third World, were of major concern to him.

Family background

Dwight David Eisenhower was born on October 14, 1890, in Denison, Texas, which was then a frontier town threatened by hostile Indians. He was the third of the seven sons, six of whom survived, who were born to David Jacob Eisenhower and Ida Elizabeth Stover Eisenhower, both of German ancestry.

In the spring of 1891, the Eisenhower family moved to Abilene, Kansas, where David worked as a mechanic in a creamery. It was not a well-paid job, and the family were poor.

"Ike," as Dwight was nicknamed from his youth, was good at sports, particularly football and baseball. He was also a good student, and in June, 1911, he won a state scholarship as a cadet to the Military Academy of West Point, New York. There he continued to excel at sports until he injured his knee playing football. He graduated with a Bachelor of Science degree in 1915.

Troops being loaded on the south coast of England ready for the D-Day invasion of occupied France in World War II.

Marriage and army service

Second Lieutenant Eisenhower was sent to Houston, Texas, for his first posting in 1915. There, he met Mamie Geneva Doud, the daughter of a retired businessman, whose family was making its annual visit to relatives in San Antonio. They were engaged on Valentine's Day, 1916, and married on July 1 of that year.

A series of army postings in the U.S., Panama and France followed. When Ike accompanied General Douglas MacArthur to the Philippines, his career as a soldier really took off. MacArthur was impressed by Eisenhower's organizing ability, and his influence determined Ike's appointment as Commanding General of the European Theater in June, 1942.

Allied Commander during World War II

During World War II, Eisenhower led "Operation Torch," the Allied landings in North Africa in 1942. After successes there, culminating in the invasion of Italy, President Truman appointed Eisenhower as Supreme Commander of the Allied Expeditionary Force in Western Europe and of "Operation Overlord," the invasion of Europe to free it from Hitler's control that took place in Normandy in June, 1944.

During the campaign, Eisenhower proved he was a great leader. He worked tactfully and successfully with the military leaders and forces of the other

As Allied Commander, Eisenhower chose June 6, 1944, as D-Day, the day on which a huge fleet of ships and thousands of planes brought millions of Allied troops onto the beaches of Normandy in northern France. A year of hard fighting followed before the Germans, under Hitler, were eventually forced back through Europe, retreating from the lands they had invaded since 1939.

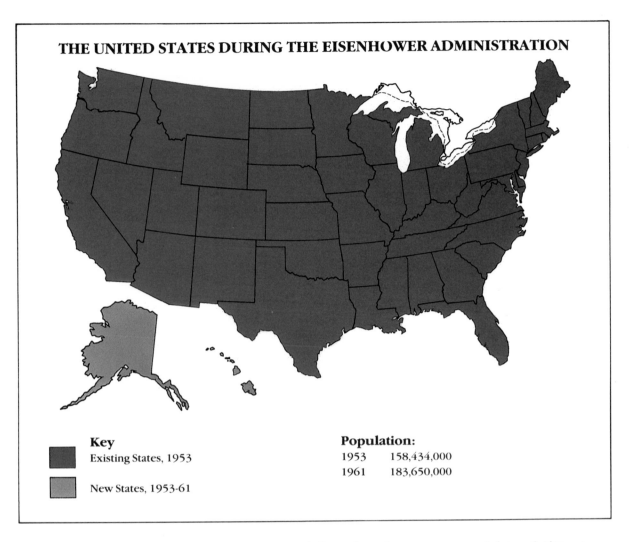

THE UNITED STATES DURING THE EISENHOWER ADMINISTRATION

Key
Existing States, 1953

New States, 1953-61

Population:
1953   158,434,000
1961   183,650,000

nations. As a soldier, he demonstrated his ability to win, overseeing strategy and tactics, and keeping the morale of the troops under his command high. It was he who received the German surrender at his military headquarters at Reims in France.

After the war

When he returned to the U.S. as a hero and a five-star general, he was appointed Chief of Staff from 1945 to 1948.

During this period, he wrote "Crusader in Europe," a book about his war experiences which became a bestseller. His experience and popularity made him a strong potential presidential candidate in the views of both the Democratic and the Republican parties.

As Allied Commander, Eisenhower meets some of the troops under his command about to fight in Operation Overlord, on D-Day.

Eisenhower did not commit himself to either party and did not wish to be considered as a candidate in 1948.

Instead, he became president of Columbia University in New York. In 1951, President Truman asked him to take command of the NATO forces in Europe. The North Atlantic Treaty Organization had been set up in 1949 by President Truman, with Britain and other West European powers, to counteract fears of aggression from the Soviet Union.

Eisenhower's concern for and interest in his men was one of the secrets of his success as a General.

First Presidential term

In 1952, Eisenhower ran as the Republican Party's presidential candidate against the Democrat, Adlai Stevenson, and won convincingly. He had promised during the campaign that he would visit Korea and see for himself the situation there.

The Korean War had been dragging on for two years with little progress and with significant American losses. It had begun in 1950 when Communist forces from North Korea had invaded

Troops were sent to South Korea under the flag of the United Nations.

South Korea. American forces under General MacArthur were sent to aid the South Korean government, and a United Nations force was deployed. After initial success, there was danger of a war with China. President Truman was not prepared to contemplate that possibility, a view which was in direct opposition to that of General MacArthur.

Truman's decision to recall MacArthur had been unpopular. The General led a body of public opinion which wanted the U.S. to adopt a more aggressive stance and use any weapons at her disposal, including atomic bombs such as those which had caused such terrifying devastation when they had been dropped on Hiroshima and Nagasaki to end World War II. When Eisenhower visited front line units and saw the situation for himself, he decided that the war must be ended to avoid the useless sacrifice of more young American men.

Despite the opposition of Dr. Syngman Rhee, the South Korean President, an armistice was signed in July, 1953. Eisenhower, like Truman, was not

Although his parents shared a religious faith and read the Bible daily, in adult life Eisenhower was not a regular churchgoer until, as President, he became a member of the National Presbyterian Church in Washington. He did believe, nevertheless, that a spiritual dimension was important in life. As leader of the American people, he encouraged them to follow his example.

prepared to use atom bombs against China and knew that without their use, China would not be defeated. It was proof of his popularity that he was able to carry through the armistice, because Congress and public opinion would not have accepted such a blow to American pride from Truman when he was president.

The problem of the use and containment of nuclear power was to remain one of the greatest issues of Eisenhower's presidency.

Atoms for peace

Early in his first term, Eisenhower gave a speech in the General Asssembly of the United Nations. He suggested that atomic energy should be used for peaceful purposes, and that Russia and America should not engage in an arms race. He wanted to "take this weapon out of the hands of the soldiers. It must be put into the hands of those who will know how ... to adapt it to the arts of peace."

He proposed that an International Atomic Agency be set up under the control of the U.N. Contributions of fissionable material from the U.S., the U.S.S.R., and the U.K. which would allow scientists from all over the world to work to find ways of harnessing atomic power to supply energy, particularly for poorer nations.

Although his speech was received enthusiastically by the 3,500 delegates and by public opinion, the Russians delayed in acting on the proposal until 1957.

The image of the mushroom-shaped cloud which follows the exploding of an atomic bomb was to become chillingly familiar despite Eisenhower's desire for the peaceful harnessing of nuclear power.

By then, it had become irrelevant because of other scientific development of hydrogen and nuclear bombs. The U.S.S.R. and the U.S. had become involved in an arms race and had stockpiled enough weapons to end the world — the very danger Eisenhower dreaded and tried to avoid.

In July, 1955, when Eisenhower met the Russian leaders, including Nikita Khrushchev, at a summit meeting in Geneva, he made another move to try to remove the fear and secrecy between the two countries. His "Open Skies" policy proposed that the U.S. and the U.S.S.R. should each have the right to inspect the other's military installations by means of aerial photography. Khrushchev refused, and another opportunity was lost.

Balancing the budget

Quite apart from his humanitarian motives, Eisenhower wanted to reduce weapons because of their enormous cost. In his election campaign, he had promised less federal interference in the affairs of individual states, as well as less federal spending. He hoped to reach a balanced budget and a reduction in taxes. He made efforts in these directions and

One reason that Eisenhower wanted four-lane highways from all major cities was to facilitate mass evacuation in the event of a Soviet nuclear attack. This expansion of the highway system had far-reaching effects on the transportation industry and on the movement of blacks from the rural South to northern and western cities.

succeeded in balancing the budget for three of his eight years in office. However, some programs involving federal spending were initiated, partly to limit the effects of a recession and partly because the Democrats held control in both Houses of Congress. In 1954, Social Security provisions were widened to include the self-employed. In 1955, the Department of Health and Welfare was set up.

McCarthyism

One of the most powerful members of the Senate was Joseph McCarthy of Wisconsin, Chairman of the Permanent Subcommittee on Investigations of the Senate Committee on Government Operations. He carried out more than 150 investigations into people in government and public life who were suspected of being members of the Communist Party. Most of his accusations were unjustified, and many people had their lives and careers ruined during his inquiries.

McCarthy became widely feared. Eisenhower, however, refused to challenge his power, saying it was beneath the dignity of a President to become involved. Only in 1954, when McCarthy began to attack members of the Army, was he censured by the Senate and his power broken.

Second term

In 1955, Eisenhower suffered a heart attack. This was followed by a major abdominal operation the next year. Despite doubts about his health, he was re-

Ike was overwhelmingly popular when elected in 1952.

WE FROM FLORIDA
BOW TO THE PEOPLE
OF WISCONSIN
for SEN. McCARTHY
Why Did
ALGER HISS
WANT TRIAL in VERMONT?
DO YOU KNOW
FLANDERS?
IF YOU
CENSURE McCARTHY
TO-DAY WILL IT BE NIXON
McCLELLAN OR IKE
TO-MORROW?

CHUSETTS
ANKS
CONSIN
McCARTH

64 QUESTION to
96 SENATORS
Who Promoted Per ss?

PREJU
COMM
PER

SEN

NEW YORK
S TO THE GREAT S
ISCONSIN
N. McCARTHY

SEN. McCARTHY
The Man Who
FULFILLED
The IKE CAMPAIGN
PROMISES

These supporters of
Senator Joseph
McCarthy regarded
him as a patriotic
American who was
rooting out
Communist spies;
others in the country
regarded his witch
hunts as
endangering civil
liberties.

Eisenhower's personal popularity guaranteed his re-election in 1956 with Richard Nixon remaining as Vice-President although the Democrats held power in Congress.

REPUBLICAN NATIONAL

elected in 1956 with a huge majority of the popular vote, although the Democrats still held power in Congress.

To counteract the effects of a recession, Congress passed the Interstate Highway Act in 1956. It authorized the building of 42,000 miles of limited access roads by 1970, paid for largely by federal funds. When the Russians launched the Sputnik space satellite in 1957, national pride was hurt. An effort was made to improve schooling and educational standards with federal financial support. The National Defense Education Act was passed in 1958 which, among other things, stressed the importance of science teaching.

Civil rights

A major topic of concern during both of Ike's administrations was that of desegregation and the securing of civil rights for American negroes. The black population had increased greatly between 1940 and 1960. Many blacks had moved from rural areas in the South to cities such as Washington, New York, Chicago and Detroit. It was much easier to organize themselves when they lived near each other. They began to voice their demands for equal rights. In the South, transportation, restaurants, theaters, beaches, and most churches were segregated. Blacks were discriminated against in housing, education, and employment. Dr. Martin Luther King, a black Baptist minister educated at Harvard, led the struggle, but preached a message of non-violence.

In his first term, Eisenhower put into effect existing laws to desegregate the armed services. He appointed some black government officers. He also appointed Earl Warren as Chief Justice of the Supreme Court. In May, 1955, the Court ruled against segregation in

The launching of Sputnik I in 1957 by the Russians was a shock to American pride.

Hawaii and Alaska became states in 1959. The St. Lawrence Seaway was opened in 1960.

In the South, blacks traditionally sat at "the back of the bus," while whites sat in the front. A campaign to desegregate public transportation was an important step in the fight for equal rights.

schools, a decision with which Eisenhower did not
privately agree. Many southern states resisted the
ruling. In Little Rock, Arkansas, in 1957, riots to stop
blacks from attending the local high school made
world headlines. Eisenhower used martial law to
enforce the Court's decision by taking over the
Arkansas National Guard and sending in paratroopers.

World peace in danger

Despite his concern about the spread of nuclear
weapons and his desire for world peace, events
toward the end of Eisenhower's presidency showed
how far there was to go to establish international
understanding, trust, and tolerance and how
committed he had become to the idea of U.S. nuclear
superiority as a deterrent to the threat of Russian
aggression.

The Eisenhower Doctrine stated that the President
could offer economic and military support to any
Middle Eastern government who asked for it to
prevent communist interference. In 1958, U.S.
Marines were sent to Lebanon at the request of
President Chamoun against his Moslem opponents. A
U.S. spy plane was shot down over Soviet territory in
May, 1960, shortly before a summit meeting was to be

held in Paris. Khrushchev refused to attend, and Eisenhower refused to apologize for the incident, admitting that such flights were part of U.S. defense policy.

There were also problems for the U.S. in Latin America. Eisenhower had supported right-wing leaders in South and Central America in a bid to keep out communist governments. In 1958, there were demonstrations in Uruguay, Peru, and Venezuela against the U.S. Vice-President Richard Nixon had to cancel the end of a goodwill tour.

In 1959, Cuban President Batista was overthrown by revolutionaries led by Fidel Castro. The U.S. recognized the new regime, but Castro's government took over major businesses, including U.S.-owned sugar plantations, and developed close links with the Soviet Union and China. Eisenhower broke off diplomatic relations near the end of his term.

In his farewell address, Eisenhower warned against the growing power of the military and the arms business in the U.S.

Later life

In retirement at his farm in Gettysburg, Pennsylvania, Ike bred Angus cattle, wrote autobiographical books, and continued to be a respected public figure. President Johnson consulted him many times regarding the Vietnam War. He died in Washington in 1969, aged seventy-eight, after a period of illness following a heart attack.

BIOGRAPHY BOX

Dwight David Eisenhower

Birthplace	Denison, Texas
Date of birth	October 14, 1890
Education	U.S. Military Academy, West Point
Profession	Soldier
Presidential term	January 20, 1953 to January 20, 1961
Party	Republican
Place of death	Washington, D.C.
Date of death	March 28, 1969
Place of burial	Abilene, Kansas

JOHN F. KENNEDY

(1913-1963)

Thirty-fifth President: 1961-1963

John F. Kennedy [signature]

Family background

John Fitzgerald Kennedy was the second of the nine children born to Rose Fitzgerald and Joseph Patrick Kennedy. Joseph was a wealthy businessman, financier, and banker who had also been U.S. Ambassador to Great Britain during Franklin D. Roosevelt's presidency. Both sides of the Kennedy family immigrated from Ireland because of a famine in the 1840s which followed the failure of the potato crop. One of John's grandfathers had been mayor of Boston; the other had served in both houses of the Massachusetts legislature. The families were Roman Catholics, and Rose was particularly devout.

John was born on May 29, 1917, in Brookline, Massachusetts. When he was thirteen, the family moved to New York, where Joseph's business interests were centered. Summers were spent in Hyannisport, Massachusetts, on Cape Cod.

After Choate School, in Wallingford, Connecticut, John attended Princeton University from 1935 to 1936. He did not complete the course; he suffered a recurrence of jaundice which he had first contracted while attending the London School of Economics in 1935. He graduated from Harvard University with a B.S. in political science in 1940. To complete his higher education, he went to Stanford University Graduate School of Business Administration in Palo Alto, California, for six months.

After touring South America, he joined the navy as an ensign. In 1943, during World War II, his torpedo boat was sunk by a Japanese destroyer. He spent fifteen hours in the water. During that time, he saved the lives of several of his crew. He was awarded the Purple Heart and the Navy and Marine Corps medal for his courage. After the war, John became a newspaper foreign correspondent in Europe, increasing his knowledge and understanding of international affairs.

Early political life

Joseph nurtured an ambition to have one of his sons become a Democratic president of the U.S. When his eldest son, Joe, was killed in the war, John became the obvious choice. Joseph used his money, power, and influence to groom and prepare John for his future role. In addition to the benefits of a good education to develop his natural intelligence, John was blessed with good looks and natural charm. He had the vision to set himself high targets and the dynamism to achieve them.

In 1946, 1948, and 1950, he was elected to the U.S. House of Representatives. In 1952, with the help of his family, who all campaigned vigorously for him, he defeated the long-serving Republican senator, Henry Cabot Lodge. Kennedy served as a senator for eight years, sitting on several important committees and gaining valuable political experience.

In 1953, he married Jacqueline Lee Bouvier, the beautiful, cultured, and intelligent daughter of John

J. F. Kennedy was the first American president born in the twentieth century, the first Roman Catholic President, and the youngest elected President.

John F. Kennedy's inauguration seemed to open up a new era of hope and idealism.

Vernon Bouvier III and Janet Lee. "Jackie," like John, came from a wealthy family, was well educated, and had traveled widely. Despite their wealth and glamour, the couple shared sadness as well as joy in their family life. They had four children: one was stillborn, one died two days after being born prematurely. The surviving children were Caroline and John. Jackie regarded bringing up her children and taking care of her husband as her major priorities, ". . . if you bungle raising your children, I don't think whatever else you do well matters very much."

John F. Kennedy was chosen as the Democratic presidential candidate in 1960 and narrowly defeated Richard Nixon in the election.

The ability to perform well on television began to be crucially important in election campaigns from the Sixties onwards.

The Kennedy era

The Kennedy family was young and attractive. Jackie brought a new sense of style and elegance to the White House. She completely refurbished it, succeeding in her aim of making it a monument to the history of the American nation. To furnish and decorate it appropriately, she set up a Fine Arts Committee to travel around the country and persuade people to donate suitable objects, which proved surprisingly successful. Another means of financing the renovation was the publication of a guide book to the White House, which the First Lady edited. She also appeared in a television program about the White House in return for a donation to the Fine Arts Committee.

The White House became a cultural as well as a social center. Ballet, chamber music, opera, and Shakespearean plays were all performed there for the entertainment of guests.

John Kennedy spoke in his inaugural address of the challenge facing the people of the United States and of the need for patriotic service. "The torch has been passed to a new generation of Americans . . . ask not what your country can do for you; ask what you can do for your country."

He chose a group of young businessmen and academics as his close advisers. His brother, Robert, who was only thirty-five, was appointed Attorney General.

Domestic policy and civil rights

Eisenhower's prime economic concern had been to balance the budget. Kennedy's priority was to stimulate growth to counteract the effects of a recession and to reduce unemployment. He reduced taxes, which had the effect of creating new jobs and increasing the output of goods produced. The Trade Expansion Act gave the president the power to cut tariffs as a retaliation against the newly organized European Economic Community.

When a steel strike was threatened, he intervened

Blacks continued to fight for their rights. It was not always easy to maintain Dr. Martin Luther King's policy of non-violence.

The window display of a Miami store during the Cuban crisis.

personally and managed to persuade the union to call it off. They accepted a pay settlement which would not cause prices to rise. Then, the steel companies put up their prices. Kennedy retaliated strongly, threatening government inquiries into their tax liabilities and price fixing. They soon gave way. Kennedy's proposals for federal spending on education and for medical insurance for retired workers over 65 were rejected by a coalition of Southern Democrats and Republicans in Congress. He did succeed with the Drugs Industry Act of 1962, a measure to increase safeguards in the manufacture

and sale of drugs, and a mental research fund.

Black Americans, under the leadership of Dr. Martin Luther King, continued to demonstrate and march to have their rights to equal education and employment opportunities put into practice. Both Robert and John Kennedy tried to support these aims, although they realized that a change of public opinion was as necessary as laws and military force. The president appointed several blacks to important government and diplomatic posts. He set up an Equal Employment Opportunities Commission and continued the policy of desegregating schools. There was significant, sometimes violent, opposition to these measures by whites, particularly in the south. Kennedy became hated in some parts of the country.

Foreign crises

Kennedy had to face humiliation early in his presidency when, in 1961, he agreed to the invasion of Cuba by a force of 1,400 Cuban exiles who intended to overthrow Fidel Castro. This C.I.A.-backed venture was badly planned, and the exiles were defeated within a day of landing in the Bay Of Pigs. The Russians made propaganda out of the fact that the U.S. had tried to interfere in the affairs of a weaker, smaller state and had failed.

Six weeks later, Kennedy and the Russian leader, Nikita Khrushchev, met at a summit conference in Vienna. There, Khrushchev delivered an ultimatum regarding Berlin. After World War II, Russia had retained control of eastern Germany. They set up the nation of East Germany, which the U.S.A. refused to recognize diplomatically as a country. The city of Berlin, in the middle of East Germany, was split into zones administered by Britain, France, the U.S. and Russia.

Khrushchev now demanded that the U.S. should legally recognize East Germany as a separate state. In addition, he wanted Berlin to continue to be governed internationally, with East Germany controlling access to it.

Dr. Martin Luther King was shot on this balcony by a white man, James Earl Ray. Jesse Jackson survived to carry on the struggle for black civil rights.

Many East Germans were escaping to the West through Berlin, which created bad publicity for the Russians. Kennedy refused to accept these terms. Both the U.S. and the U.S.S.R. increased their military spending as tension increased. The Russians built a wall of concrete and barbed wire, which divided Berlin into East and West. The U.S. did not try to remove it, but 1,500 Allied troops traveled down the autobahn from West Germany to West Berlin to demonstrate the West's determination to support West Berlin. Eventually, the crisis petered out in a stalemate. The wall remained.

The greatest test of Kennedy's will to contain Russian expansion came in October, 1962. American spy planes had discovered that the Russians were building missile sites in Cuba, on the American doorstep, and arming them with hydrogen warheads. Their operation would reduce the warning time of a nuclear attack on the U.S. from fifteen minutes to two. Kennedy ordered that all ships approaching Cuba were to be searched for weapons. He demanded that the sites be dismantled and the missiles removed. He also warned that any missile attacks on the West would trigger massive retaliation on the Soviet Union by the U.S.

People across the western world waited apprehensively on October 24 as Russian ships, sailing to Cuba and believed to be carrying missiles, stopped

BIOGRAPHY BOX

John Fitzgerald Kennedy

Birthplace	Brookline, Massachusetts
Date of birth	May 29, 1917
Education	Harvard
Profession	Politician
Presidential term	January 20, 1961 to November 22, 1963
Party	Democratic
Place of death	Dallas, Texas
Date of death	November 22, 1963
Place of burial	Arlington National Cemetery

in mid-ocean. Two days later, Kennedy received a letter from Khrushchev agreeing to dismantle the missile sites in return for an American pledge not to invade Cuba. This was agreed, and by November, all the missiles were gone.

Following the defusing of this crisis, both Khrushchev and Kennedy felt able to enter negotiations to limit the testing of atomic bombs, which led to the Test Ban Treaty of 1963 signed by the U.S., the U.K. and the U.S.S.R. This agreement stopped the testing of bombs in the atmosphere, underwater, and in space. Also, a direct land communication link, or "Hot Line," was set up between the leaders in Moscow and Washington; it had taken four hours for messages to be passed during the Cuban crisis.

Space

Kennedy regarded the exploration of space as important for the country. Despite its great cost, it provided a target and a focus for the nation. Success would mean great international prestige. It was also a useful way of increasing employment and scientific knowledge. In April, 1961, the Russian, Yuri Gagarin,

John Kennedy declared to Congress that an American astronaut would stand on the Moon by 1970.

THE UNITED STATES DURING THE KENNEDY ADMINISTRATION

Key
States

Population:
1961   183,650,000
1963   190,417,000

had been the first man in space, flying 188 miles above the earth for 108 minutes in Vostok 1. Kennedy was determined that the first man on the moon would be an American. He asked Congress for an extra $7-9,000,000.00 over five years to pay for research. In 1962, John Glenn was the first American to orbit the earth.

Dallas

In November, 1963, the President was in Dallas, Texas, campaigning for the next election. As the motorcade drove past the Texas School Book Depository, Kennedy was shot and fatally wounded. He was pronounced dead half an hour later at the Parkland Memorial Hospital. An employee of the Book

Depository, Lee Harvey Oswald, was immediately arrested for the murder. Oswald himself was later shot dead by Jack Ruby, a local nightclub owner, while being transferred to another jail.

Both murders were seen by television viewers around the world. They caused horror, disbelief, and great sadness. Great hopes for the future had been blown away. There was also anxiety that the Russians or the Cubans might have been involved in a conspiracy: Oswald was a Marxist, a previous defector to the Soviet Union, and he was trying to get political asylum in Cuba. Ordinary people across the world grieved as they watched the funeral and burial in Arlington National Cemetery in Washington.

Vice-President Johnson was sworn in and set up a massive investigation into the assassination. He wanted it completed before the 1964 elections, and some people thought it was not thorough enough. The conclusion was that Oswald had acted alone and had not been part of a conspiracy. This verdict is still being disputed by some researchers.

John Kennedy's grave at the Arlington National Cemetery.

The shooting of Lee
Harvey Oswald by
Jack Ruby was seen
on television by
millions.

LYNDON B. JOHNSON
(1908-1973)

Thirty-sixth President: 1963-1969

Lyndon B. Johnson, the Vice-President who became
President following the murder of John F. Kennedy in
Dallas in 1963, had a very different background and
personality from his predecessor. He was a tall Texan
of humble origins with a loud voice and a forthright
manner. He was also a very experienced politician,
who was determined to carry on and put into effect
the program of social and civil reform which John
Kennedy had initiated.

Family and early life

Lyndon Baines Johnson was born near Stonewall,
Gillespie County, Texas, in 1908. He was raised in
Johnson City, a small town founded by his
grandfather. Both his father, a struggling cotton
farmer, and his grandfather had served in the state
legislature. On leaving the local high school in 1924,
Lyndon worked on a road gang in California. After
three years of similar jobs, he decided to be a teacher
and enrolled at Southwest Texas State Teachers
College. He did not really enjoy teaching. After two
years, he became secretary in 1932 to R. M. Kleburg, a
Texas congressman, and moved to Washington with
him.

In 1934, he met and married Claudia Alta Taylor,
nicknamed Lady Bird, who was also a Texan and a

graduate in arts and journalism from the University of Texas. They had two daughters, Lynda Bird and Luci Baines, who were married at the White House during the Johnson administration.

Lady Bird campaigned actively for her husband. As First Lady, she set out to beautify the nation's capital with trees and plants, a project which became countrywide. She was also very active in the President's program to help the poor and was particularly interested in the Head Start project to provide preschool education for poor children.

Political career

In 1935, during Franklin D. Roosevelt's presidency, Lyndon Johnson was appointed as the Texas director of the New Deal's National Youth Administration. He was successful in the job, which involved creating part-time employment for poor high school and college students. He became a Democratic member of the U.S. House of Representatives in 1937 and served until 1949, except for war service in the Navy in 1942. He supported Franklin D. Roosevelt and his New Deal and remained deeply committed to the cause of improving the lives of the poor and underprivileged throughout his political career.

He became a Senator in 1949, serving on the Armed Services and Appropriations Committees. He was chosen as Senate Minority Leader in 1953 and became Majority Leader the next year when the Democrats gained control of the Senate. He generally worked with the Republican President Eisenhower rather than against him, putting the interests of the country before short-term party advantage.

In 1960, having earned a reputation as an effective and energetic politician, he accepted the vice-

> During Johnson's presidency, Martin Luther King and Robert Kennedy were both killed by gunmen.

Lyndon Johnson was sworn in as President on board Air Force One after President Kennedy's assassination in Dallas.

presidential nomination under John F. Kennedy.
Johnson's strenuous campaigning in the South was an
important factor in the narrow Democratic victory
over the Republican candidate, Richard Nixon.
Johnson was an energetic vice-president, taking a
particularly active role in developing America's space
program. In April, 1961, he visited Vietnam on
President Kennedy's behalf and advised on his return
that the U.S. should defend South Vietnam and the
government of Ngo Dinh Diem.

Johnson as President

Johnson took the presidential oath of office at Dallas
Airport and assumed control. President Kennedy had
submitted to Congress many bills which had not been
debated. Johnson made it one of his first priorities to
continue Kennedy's programs for social reform to
help the poor and underprivileged, and in the field of
civil rights.

President Johnson signs the Civil Rights Act of 1964.

An experienced and capable politician, Johnson was able to steer many of these measures through Congress and so bring to fruition some of Kennedy's dreams. The Civil Rights Act, passed in June, 1964, dealt with voting and employment rights for blacks and forbade segregation in public places.

Johnson was elected president in his own right in 1964 with a large majority over the right-wing Republican candidate, Senator Barry Goldwater. Large Democratic majorities in both houses of Congress generally supported his policies.

The great society

Johnson spoke of his aim to build a Great Society, "a place where the city of man serves not only the needs of the body and the demands of commerce, but the desire for beauty and the hunger for community."

He said, "We can open the doors of learning, of fruitful labor and rewarding leisure, not just to the

Blacks and whites marched together in protest against discrimination in civil rights.

privileged few but . . . to everyone.''

Nevertheless, he had inherited the beginnings of a time of violence and unrest. Although Dr. Martin Luther King preached a policy of non-violent protest against racial discrimination, a new generation of black leaders such as Malcolm X and Eldridge Cleaver, the Black Panther Leader, promoted violence as a legitimate means of achieving equality. When Martin Luther King was shot dead by James Earl Ray, a white man, the violence increased.

Blacks tended to live in poor and crowded conditions in cities, and there were race riots during

Martin Luther King had a meeting with President Johson in August 1965.

the hot summers of Johnson's administration. In 1964, it was Harlem; in 1965, the Watts district of Los Angeles; in 1967, Detroit. Newark, Cleveland, and Chicago also suffered. Many people died — at least 40 in Detroit — and 8,000 National Guardsmen supported by 5,000 paratroopers were called in to quell the disorder.

The Voting Rights Act of 1965 enabled the Civil Rights Act to be enforced. It gave the Attorney General the power to order federal registrars to check that all the eligible voters had been registered in a state. As a result, many more blacks added their names to the electoral rolls in some southern states. It meant that future political leaders in these states had to moderate their racial policies in order to get the blacks to vote for them.

Johnson also promised to make war on poverty. During his presidency, there was increased spending on health, education, and welfare. Imaginative schemes initiated by the new Office of Economic Opportunity, such as Volunteers for Service in America, the Community Action Program, the Neighborhood Youth Corps, and Upward Bound, encouraged the poor to help themselves and each other. Large tax cuts encouraged a booming economy. Johnson also succeeded in getting the Medical Care Act passed in 1965. It provided some government health care for the old and the poor, paid for by federal funds and taxes on employers.

The Housing and Urban Development Act of 1965 was part of the Johnsons' campaign to "Beautify America." Acts to preserve national wildernesses, to control water quality and waste disposal, to beautify land along highways, and to set up the Redwood National Park were also passed.

Vietnam

Despite all these real and positive achievements, Johnson is mainly remembered as the president under whom the United States fought the Vietnam War. Kennedy had sent about 14,000 servicemen as

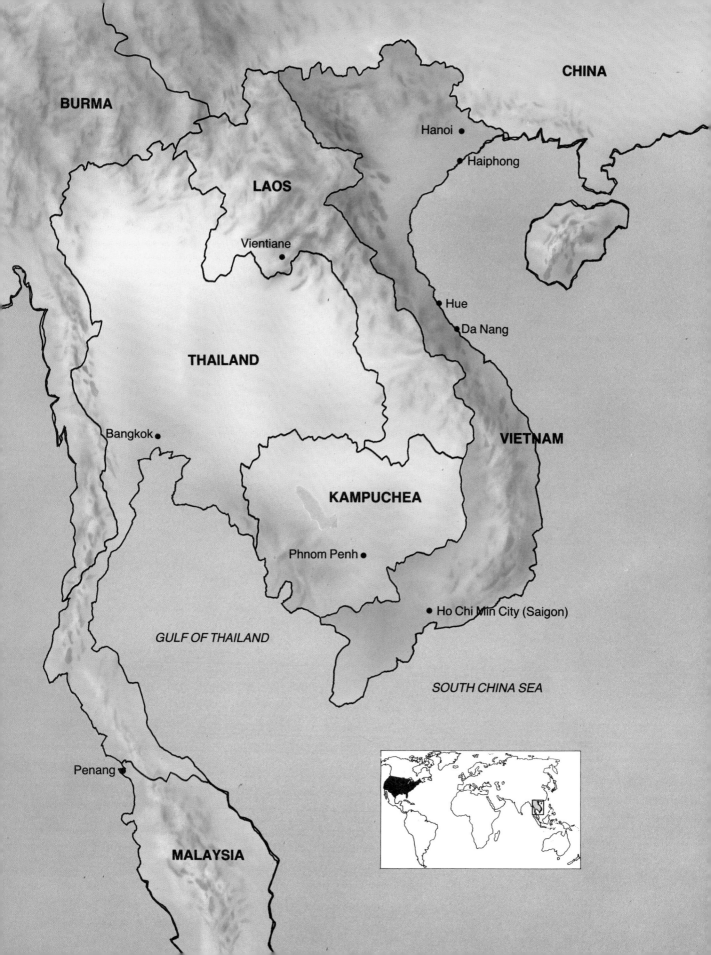

CHINA

BURMA

Hanoi •

LAOS

• Haiphong

Vientiane
•

THAILAND

• Hue

• Da Nang

Bangkok •

VIETNAM

KAMPUCHEA

Phnom Penh •

Ho Chi Min City (Saigon)
•

GULF OF THAILAND

SOUTH CHINA SEA

Penang •

MALAYSIA

The issue of America's involvement in the Vietnam War divided public opinion.

"advisers" to help the South Vietnamese government under Ngo Dinh Diem against Vietcong guerrillas who were trying to unite the country under the communist government of Ho Chi Minh. The U.S. government was concerned that a communist government in Vietnam would lead to the spread of Soviet influence across Southeast Asia.

Johnson felt he had to take a tough line and that the quickest way to end the war was to bomb North Vietnam as heavily as possible. In February, 1965, Johnson ordered the bombing. In March, American Marines went into combat. The numbers of young men drafted to fight in Vietnam increased rapidly. By the end of Johnson's presidency, over 500,000 troops were there. Nearly 250,000 American servicemen were killed or injured during the course of the war.

The war turned into a disaster for Johnson. The U.S. did not dare to use all its bombing power for fear of provoking Soviet or Chinese retaliation on behalf of North Vietnam. In any case, bombing alone would not win the war. Vietnam was a rural, not an industrial, country. American soldiers were needed to defend U.S. air bases in South Vietnam. As in all wars, innocent civilians and children suffered as much as the troops. In this case, the horrors were televised. The American

This map shows Vietnam and her neighbors. The inset map shows the position of Indo China in relation to the U.S.

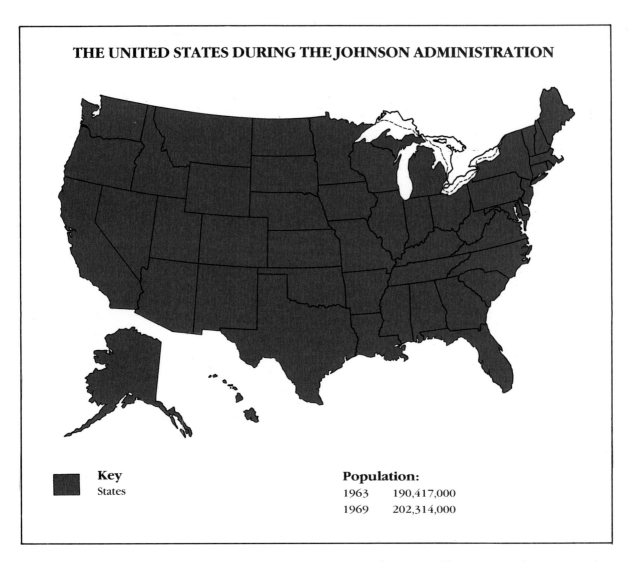

THE UNITED STATES DURING THE JOHNSON ADMINISTRATION

Key
States

Population:

1963	190,417,000
1969	202,314,000

nation could not pretend to itself, as people in similar situations had been able to do in earlier times, that the war was not happening. There was widespread condemnation of the war. Many young men left the country to avoid being drafted and forced to serve in Vietnam. Protests and demonstrations against U.S. policy gave rise to slogans such as, "Hey, hey, L.B.J., how many kids did you kill today?"

After a successful offensive by the Vietcong in 1968, Johnson ordered a partial halt to the bombing. Peace talks began in Paris.

Retirement

When he appeared on television on March 31, 1968,

to announce the reduction of bombing in Vietnam, Johnson also announced that he would not run for re-election. He had worked very hard, but he had lost support in the country and among his own party. Lady Bird was concerned about his health, following a gall bladder operation. The couple retired to their ranch in Texas and lived there quietly until Johnson's death from a heart attack in 1973.

For the first time the daily horrors and atrocities of war were brought into the family living room by means of television.

BIOGRAPHY BOX

Lyndon Baines Johnson

Birthplace	Stonewall, Texas
Date of birth	August 27, 1908
Education	Southwest Texas State Teachers College
Profession	Public administrator
Presidential term	November 22, 1963 to January 20, 1969
Party	Democratic
Place of death	San Antonio, Texas
Date of death	January 22, 1973
Place of burial	Johnson City, Texas

GLOSSARY

Allies — Britain, France, the U.S.S.R., and those European countries which opposed Germany in the two World Wars

bill — A suggested law; when a bill has been passed, it becomes an act

cabinet — A small group of appointed government officials who advise the president and decide what the government should do

delegate — A representative sent to a conference

federal — Relating to the central government of a group of states who have agreed to unite, as distinct from the governments of the individual states

financier — Someone who makes money by borrowing, lending, and selling money

fissionable materials — Elements such as uranium and plutonium which can be used for making nuclear weapons

guerrillas — Fighters who attack suddenly from secret hiding places instead of as a regular army fighting organized battles

legislature — The part of a country's government which makes its laws

Marxist — A follower of Karl Marx who believes that individuals should not own property and that the state should provide work and the means of life for everyone

political asylum — Being allowed to enter a country in order to escape persecution because of political beliefs

satellite — Body in orbit around another body, such as the moon around the earth

segregation — Keeping people of different races apart by sending them to separate schools and providing separate public facilities

tariff — A law imposing customs duties on exports and imports. In the United States in the nineteenth and twentieth centuries, the tariff was used to protect home industry from foreign competition.

Third World — The countries of Africa, Asia, and Latin America which are politically independent of both communist and western nations. They are generally poor and underdeveloped, and the phrase is often used to mean this.

INDEX